# Lifecharge PowerPAC

## Principles, Applications and Charts

## By
## Scott L. Newberger MBA, MA, CMC

*Where there is no vision, the people perish*
-Proverbs 29:18

# Table of Contents

# How to use this book

In today's fast paced world, where change happens quickly and frequently, time is at a premium. Yet self improvement, fulfillment and growth are still very important to most people. Many individuals want to learn how to develop personally and achieve goals. This book may be considered a guide or handbook to facilitate self analysis as well as examine how one interacts with others and his or her environment. It can then assist to define one's purpose and create goals to achieve through mental imagery and other strategies.

The book is arranged in bullet format with applications for each concept, as well as charts and worksheets to allow rapid comprehension of principles. It can be read from front to back, immediately or over time, while related activities are completed along the way. This may be the most effective way to gain better personal insight and then set and achieve goals that are important. However, it can also be used as a reference book to learn about certain principles when desired and to complete activities that can help one grasp individual concepts and cultivate new skills.

Worksheets are designed to facilitate learning by applying principles directly to one's own circumstances. When completing worksheets, ample space is provided to fill in each field completely. However, filling in each field is not necessary to benefit from using the worksheet. Individuals can fill in some of the fields or use the worksheets as desired to learn and apply principles as each situation demands. The worksheets can be revisited later for further completion or new worksheets may be started based on more recent information.

This book was created to provide a quick and comprehensive way to learn how to gain a greater introspective insight, build a mission and vision statement as well as set and achieve meaningful goals that can change lives in a positive way. It is hoped that all who learn from it may grow and reach a high level of achievement.

# POWER PRINCIPLES

# POWER PRINCIPLE 1:

**Each individual has inherent worth and possesses infinite potential.**

- Absolute essential initial principle to which you must gain a conviction, all others will assimilate.

- A realization of inherent characteristic strengths, resources and opportunities is an important element of this principle.

- Some people are only restricted by their own misguided erroneous self-concept.

- When you come to the realization of the magnificence of each human being, you appreciate yourself and others more. This will engender respect for others, their worth, and complexity.

- If you don't believe in yourself, you should learn to love yourself and have a hope to believe.

Application:

Create list of your positive qualities and attributes. Refrain from including negative aspects at this time. There will be an opportunity to consider those during analysis.

# Powerful Positives

Create a list of your positive qualities and attributes.

_____

_____

_____

_____

_____

_____

_____

_____

_____

_____

_____

_____

_____

_____

_____

_____

_____

_____

_____

_____

_____

_____

_____

_____

# POWER PRINCIPLE 2:

**Individuals have the power to change, progress and use their resources to create the future they desire.**

- There are opportunities *now* that can affect the future.

- Each person has the characteristics and resources to meet with opportunities to achieve success.

- Despite past performance or accomplishments an individual has the power to accomplish and become what they once considered impossible.

- **Now** is the time to begin, you must live your new life and dreams now.

Application:

Challenge traditionally held beliefs, patterns of thought, assumptions and behavior that inhibit new growth or change within your life. Don't forget to include counterproductive habits and practices. Begin to believe that you can change and become what you would like.

# Challenge for Change

Make a list of traditionally held beliefs, patterns of thought,
assumptions and behaviors that inhibit new growth or change.
Check each box when the perspective has changed or the item has been challenged.

☐ _____
_____

☐ _____
_____

☐ _____
_____

☐ _____
_____

☐ _____
_____

☐ _____
_____

☐ _____
_____

☐ _____
_____

☐ _____
_____

☐ _____
_____

# POWER PRINCIPLE 3:

## The Whole Individual

- Each person is a complex individual, made up of mental, emotional, physical and spiritual characteristics.

  1. **Mental**- Mental characteristics refer to your intellect, knowledge, mind function and mental capabilities.

  2. **Emotional**- Feelings, passions, likes, dislikes, personal preferences and the way an individual displays them encompass the Emotional characteristic of an individual.

  3. **Physical**- The physical body, as well as the influence of the physical traits of a person on other characteristics, people and the environment is considered the physical characteristic.

  4. **Spiritual**- Spiritual aspects of a person are related to the force that gives life to our being. Some consider their relationship to Deity, as well as how they relate to their own spirit a large part of spirituality. Others feel the sense of what inherently is right or wrong, good or evil drives their spirituality.

- Each complex individual interacts with others interpersonally and with their environment. Within the Whole Individual Theory, these exchanges are usually referred to as interactions and are described in the following way:

1. **Interpersonal**- How someone relates to and connects with others is considered interpersonal interactions in reference to the Whole Individual Theory.

2. **Environmental**- The interaction with the environment deals with the interrelationships between a person and their environment. The influence of an individual on his or her surroundings, as well as the influence of the surroundings on the individual is included here.

- To progress, each person should analyze some or all of their characteristics and possible interactions and use them when given opportunities to achieve productive purposes.

- The Whole Individual characteristics and interactions relate to and interact with one another. The proper balance of these characteristics and the management of interactions with others and the environment lead to fulfillment and productivity.

Application:

Study and understand the characteristics and interactions of the Whole Individual Theory. Consider how they apply to your life.

# POWER PRINCIPLE 3:
## The Whole Individual

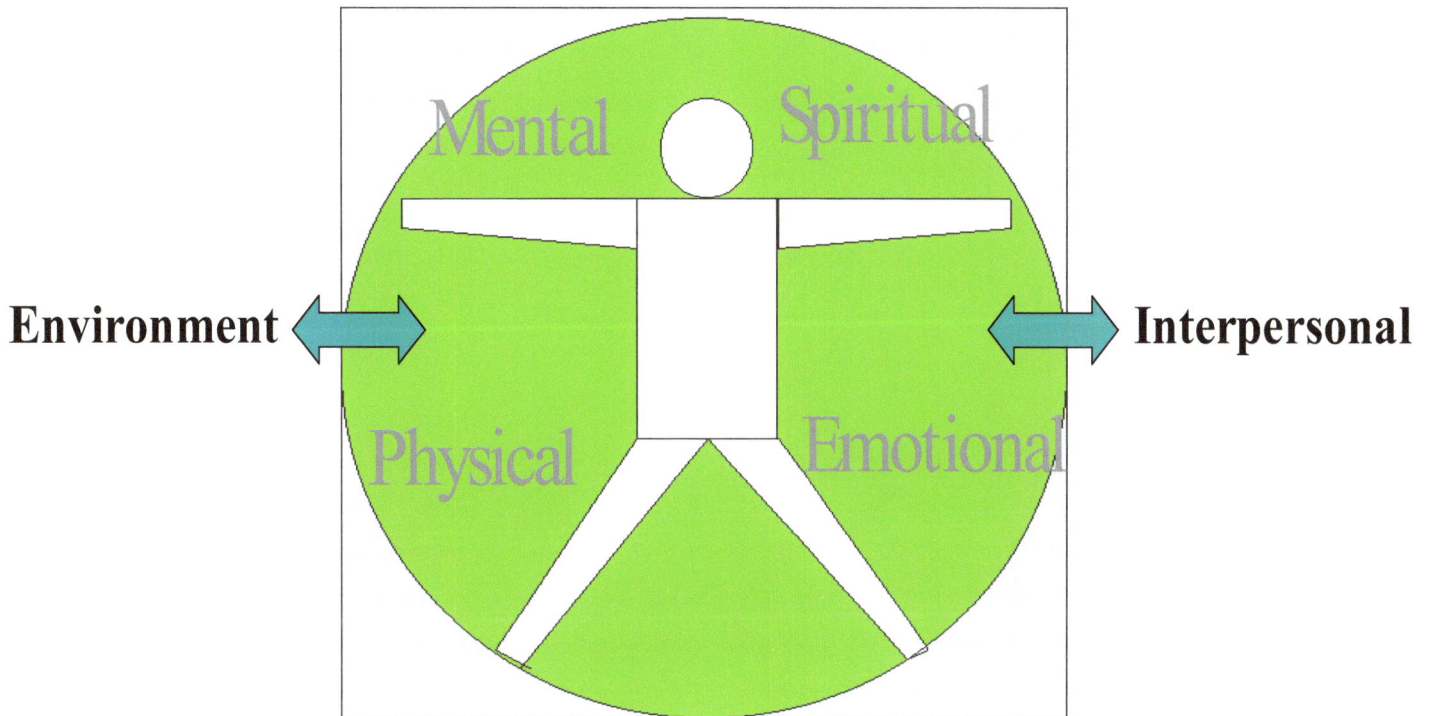

Mental   Spiritual

**Environment** ⟷     ⟷ **Interpersonal**

Physical   Emotional

# POWER PRINCIPLE 4:

## Self Assessment through "SCODD Analysis"

- "SCODD Analysis"- Strengths, Challenges, Opportunities, Dangers and Desires.

A self assessment should be done through an analysis of any or all of the characteristics and interactions based on the following:

- **Strengths**- What inherent or developed capabilities in each characteristic or interaction may be employed to reach what is desired?

- **Challenges**- Inherent or developed shortcomings that could inhibit the achievement of goals if not addressed, overcome or avoided.

   1. With diligence to improve, some challenges may be turned into strengths.

   2. Challenges should not be seen as things that would prohibit achieving or being what is desired. They should be viewed as obstacles to be overcome, improved upon or avoided.

   3. Each challenge should be analyzed to determine if it should be overcome and what it will take to do so, or if it should be avoided in order to accomplish the overall purpose.

- **Opportunities**- Occasions may arise, or be discovered in which strengths or desires may be maximized that will propel an individual towards achieving his or her overall purpose.

- **Dangers**- Risks or hazards that may inhibit the ability to use strengths to maximize opportunities. Such situations need to be identified and evaluated so appropriate action may be taken to minimize or eliminate the danger.

- **Desires**- What an individual personally wants for themselves when considering each characteristic and interaction is a vital element of the "SCODD Analysis."

    1. What is desired should be based on what is valued within each characteristic or interaction.

    2. Determining what's desired, based on what's valued, helps to provide inherent motivation to achieve what is really important.

- When a "SCODD Analysis" is done it enables you to understand where you stand with respect to each characteristic, interaction and as a whole.

- A "SCODD Analysis" may shed light on what is most important to you, and where you might be out of balance.

Application:
Conduct a "SCODD Analysis" to identify some of your strengths, challenges, opportunities, dangers and desires within any or all of your characteristics or interactions. Although you may not fill out all of the fields, space is given to be as comprehensive as desired.

# "SCODD Analysis" Worksheet
## MENTAL

Strengths: _____
_____
_____
_____

Challenges: _____
_____
_____
_____

Opportunities: _____
_____
_____
_____

Dangers: _____
_____
_____
_____

Desires: _____
_____
_____
_____

# "SCODD Analysis" Worksheet

## EMOTIONAL

Strengths: _____
_____
_____
_____

Challenges: _____
_____
_____
_____

Opportunities: _____
_____
_____
_____

Dangers: _____
_____
_____
_____

Desires: _____
_____
_____
_____

# "SCODD Analysis" Worksheet
## PHYSICAL

Strengths: _____
_____
_____
_____

Challenges: _____
_____
_____
_____

Opportunities: _____
_____
_____
_____

Dangers: _____
_____
_____
_____

Desires: _____
_____
_____
_____

# "SCODD Analysis" Worksheet

## SPIRITUAL

Strengths: _____

_____

_____

_____

Challenges: _____

_____

_____

_____

Opportunities: _____

_____

_____

_____

Dangers: _____

_____

_____

_____

Desires: _____

_____

_____

_____

# "SCODD Analysis" Worksheet

## INTERPERSONAL

Strengths: _____
_____
_____
_____

Challenges: _____
_____
_____
_____

Opportunities: _____
_____
_____
_____

Dangers: _____
_____
_____
_____

Desires: _____
_____
_____
_____

# "SCODD Analysis" Worksheet

## ENVIRONMENTAL

Strengths: _____

_____

_____

_____

Challenges: _____

_____

_____

_____

Opportunities: _____

_____

_____

_____

Dangers: _____

_____

_____

_____

Desires: _____

_____

_____

_____

# POWER PRINCIPLE 5:

**Based on the "SCODD Analysis," and values, create a vision and Mission statement.**

A Vision Statement:

- Defines who or what you are or will be.
- Is short, succinct and easy to remember.
- Describes a person in terms of their strengths, opportunities and values.
- Should elicit a clear, graphic picture of what you want to be.
- Helps to define the mission statement.
- Visions may change and adapt based on the time frame and current circumstances.

A Mission Statement:

- Clearly defines your purpose.
- Explains how you will achieve your vision using strengths, opportunities and desire.
- Describes what may be employed to achieve a goal.

Application:

Create and write out a mission and vision statement based on your "SCODD Analysis" and values.

# Mission and Vision Creation

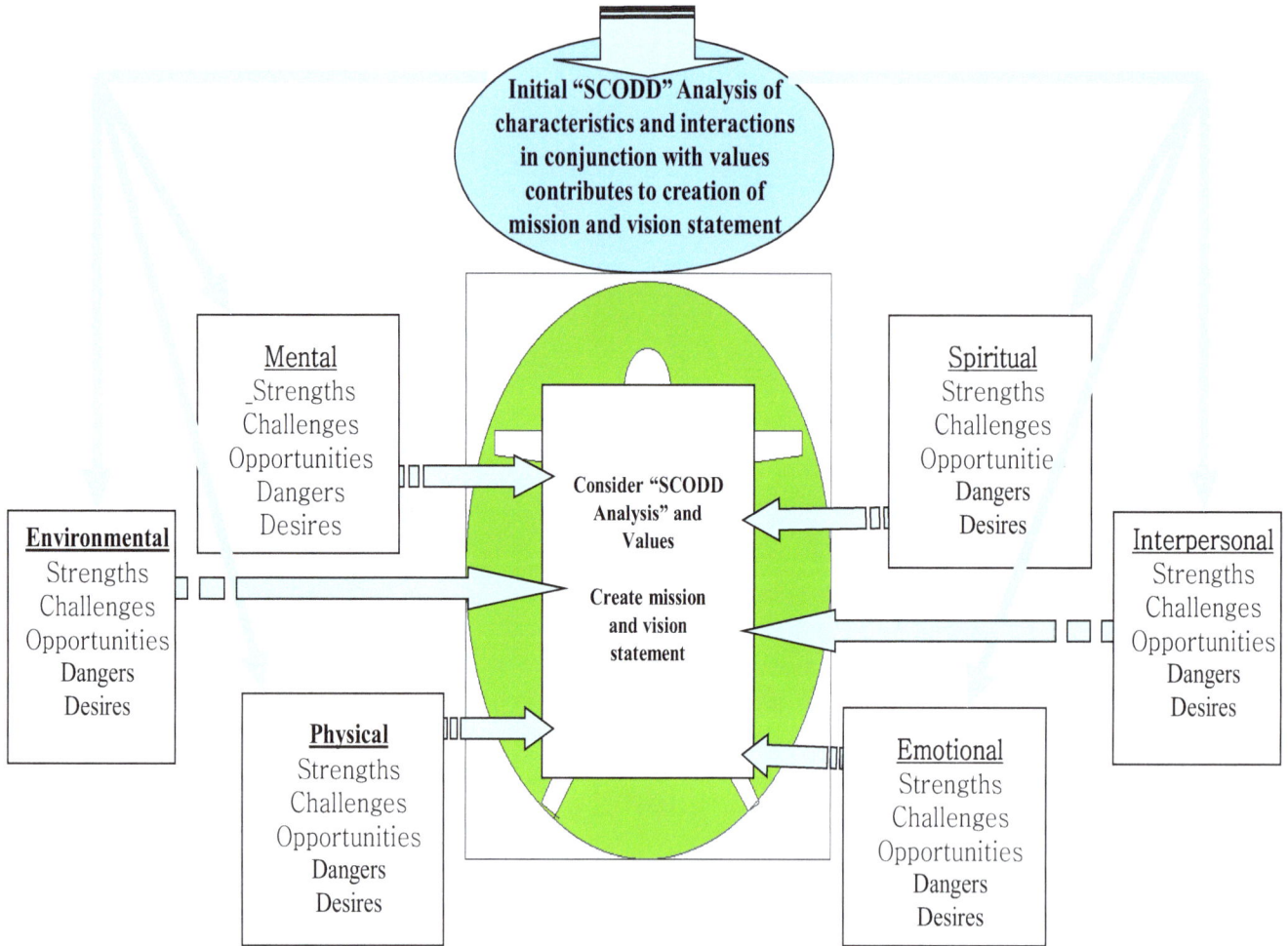

Initial "SCODD" Analysis of characteristics and interactions in conjunction with values contributes to creation of mission and vision statement

Mental
Strengths
Challenges
Opportunities
Dangers
Desires

Spiritual
Strengths
Challenges
Opportunitie
Dangers
Desires

Environmental
Strengths
Challenges
Opportunities
Dangers
Desires

Interpersonal
Strengths
Challenges
Opportunities
Dangers
Desires

Consider "SCODD Analysis" and Values

Create mission and vision statement

Physical
Strengths
Challenges
Opportunities
Dangers
Desires

Emotional
Strengths
Challenges
Opportunities
Dangers
Desires

# Value Worksheet

Make a prioritized list of what is important to YOU. Examples may be family, religion, career, education, etc. This list can help you understand what you value.

1. _____

_____

2. _____

_____

3. _____

_____

4. _____

_____

5. _____

_____

6. _____

_____

7. _____

_____

# Vision and Mission Statement

## Create a mission and vision statement based on your "SCODD Analysis" and values.

## Vision Statement:

- Defines who or what you are or will be.
- Is short, succinct and easy to remember.
- Describes a person in terms of their strengths, opportunities and values.
- Should elicit a clear, graphic picture of what you want to be.
- Helps to define the mission statement.
- Visions may change and adapt based on the time frame and current circumstances.

_____

_____

_____

_____

_____

_____

_____

_____

_____

_____

## Mission Statement:

- Clearly defines your purpose.
- Explains how you will achieve your vision using strengths, opportunities and desire.
- Describes what may be employed to achieve a goal.

_____

_____

_____

_____

_____

_____

_____

# "SCODD Analysis" leads to values, vision and mission

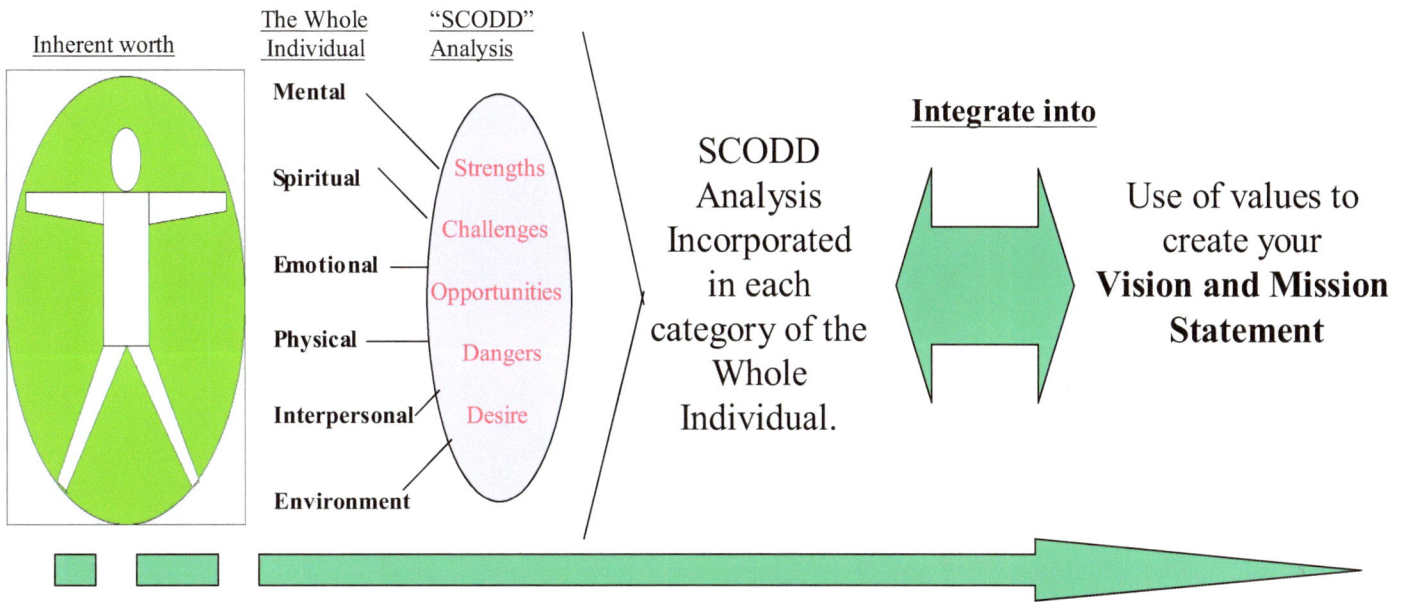

Inherent worth

The Whole Individual
- Mental
- Spiritual
- Emotional
- Physical
- Interpersonal
- Environment

"SCODD" Analysis
- Strengths
- Challenges
- Opportunities
- Dangers
- Desire

SCODD Analysis Incorporated in each category of the Whole Individual.

Integrate into

Use of values to create your **Vision and Mission Statement**

# POWER PRINCIPLE 6:

**Formulate goals based on the "SCODD Analysis," mission and vision statements. Prioritize them based on the mission and vision statements and define them based on the Whole Individual Theory.**

Formation of Goals:

- Should be based on a "SCODD Analysis" and vision and mission statements. This allows goals that integrate the analysis of a present state with the declared desired state.

- Goals can be more effective if they are written, have an assigned time frame and can be measured.

Prioritization of Goals:

- Once goals have been created, it should be determined which will promote the mission to achieve the vision the most quickly, efficiently and/or effectively. This goal should be worked on first.

- Accomplishment of the highest priority goal may help complete other goals, which will further facilitate your mission to reach your vision.

Definition of Goals:

- Goals may be defined more completely using the characteristics and interactions of the Whole Individual Theory as follows:

**Mentally**- Completely define your goal; envision in your *mind* what your goal will be like, and what you will be thinking when you accomplish it.

•**Emotionally**-What will be your *emotions* when you accomplish your goal? How will this affect you and others?

•**Physically**- Envision what you will be doing *physically* when you accomplish your goal and how it will feel *physically*. What will you feel, see, smell and hear?

•**Spiritually**- what will be your experience *spiritually* when you accomplish your goal? How will this affect you and others *spiritually*?

•**Interpersonally**-Who will be present when you accomplish your goal? How will your accomplishment affect others and your *interactions* with them?

•**Environmentally**-What will surround you when you accomplish your goal? What will be the sights, sounds, smells, and feelings of the *environment*?

- Once a goal is made, it can be broken down into Intermediate goals and short term steps that need to be accomplished in accordance with the mission. This will help keep focus on the goal while assisting with incremental progress towards accomplishment.

- Progress with short term steps and intermediate goals builds motivation to continue until the long range goal is achieved.

- Keep track of the progress of short term steps, Intermediate goals and your long range goal. A chart, daily planner or task list may be helpful with this.

Application:

Create and write out goals based on your "SCODD Analysis," vision and mission. Prioritize your goals according to which will help attain your mission and vision the most quickly, efficiently and effectively with the Goal List. You may more clearly define your goals as they relate to your characteristics and interactions using the Goal Definition. Finally a goal may be broken down into intermediate goals and short term steps using the goal worksheet.

# Goal List

Based on your "SCODD Analysis" and values, create and list goals. Prioritize them based on which will help facilitate your mission and vision the most effectively and efficiently.

☐ _____
_____ **Priority#** _____

☐ _____
_____ **Priority#** _____

☐ _____
_____ **Priority#** _____

☐ _____
_____ **Priority#** _____

☐ _____
_____ **Priority#** _____

☐ _____
_____ **Priority#** _____

☐ _____
_____ **Priority#** _____

☐ _____
_____ **Priority#** _____

# Goal Definition

### Select and define your highest priority goal(s) based on characteristics and interactions. Continue with the goal next in priority.

## GOAL: _____     Date to be achieved _____

_____

_____

**Mentally**- Completely define your goal; envision in your *mind* what your goal will be like, and what you will be thinking.

_____

_____

**Emotionally**-What will be your *emotions* when you reach your goal? How will it affect you and others?

_____

_____

**Physically**- Envision what you will be doing *physically* when you accomplish your goal and how it will feel *physically*. What will you feel, see, smell and hear?

_____

_____

**Spiritually**- what will be your experience *spiritually* when you accomplish your goal? How will this affect you and others *spiritually*?

_____

_____

**Interpersonally**-Who will be present when you accomplish your goal? How will your accomplishment affect others and your *interactions* with them?

_____

_____

**Environmentally**-What will surround you when you accomplish your goal? What will be the sights, sounds, smells, and feelings of the *environment*?

_____

_____

# Goal Worksheet

Select and clarify your highest priority goal(s) with intermediate goals and short term steps. Continue with the goal next in priority.

## GOAL: _____ Date to be Achieved _____

☐ _____

_____

## Intermediate Goals

☐ _____

_____

☐ _____

_____

## Short Term Steps

☐ _____

_____

☐ _____

_____

☐ _____

_____

# POWER PRINCIPLE 7:

**Use the Whole Individual characteristics and interactions as resources to achieve goals.**

- Mental

- Emotional

- Physical

- Spiritual

- Interpersonal

- Environmental

Application:

Use the inherent characteristics and interactions to help achieve the goal. In the Methods and Strategies section, there are techniques that may be used to effectively leverage characteristics and interactions to achieve success.

# "SCODD Analysis" and Goal Formulation

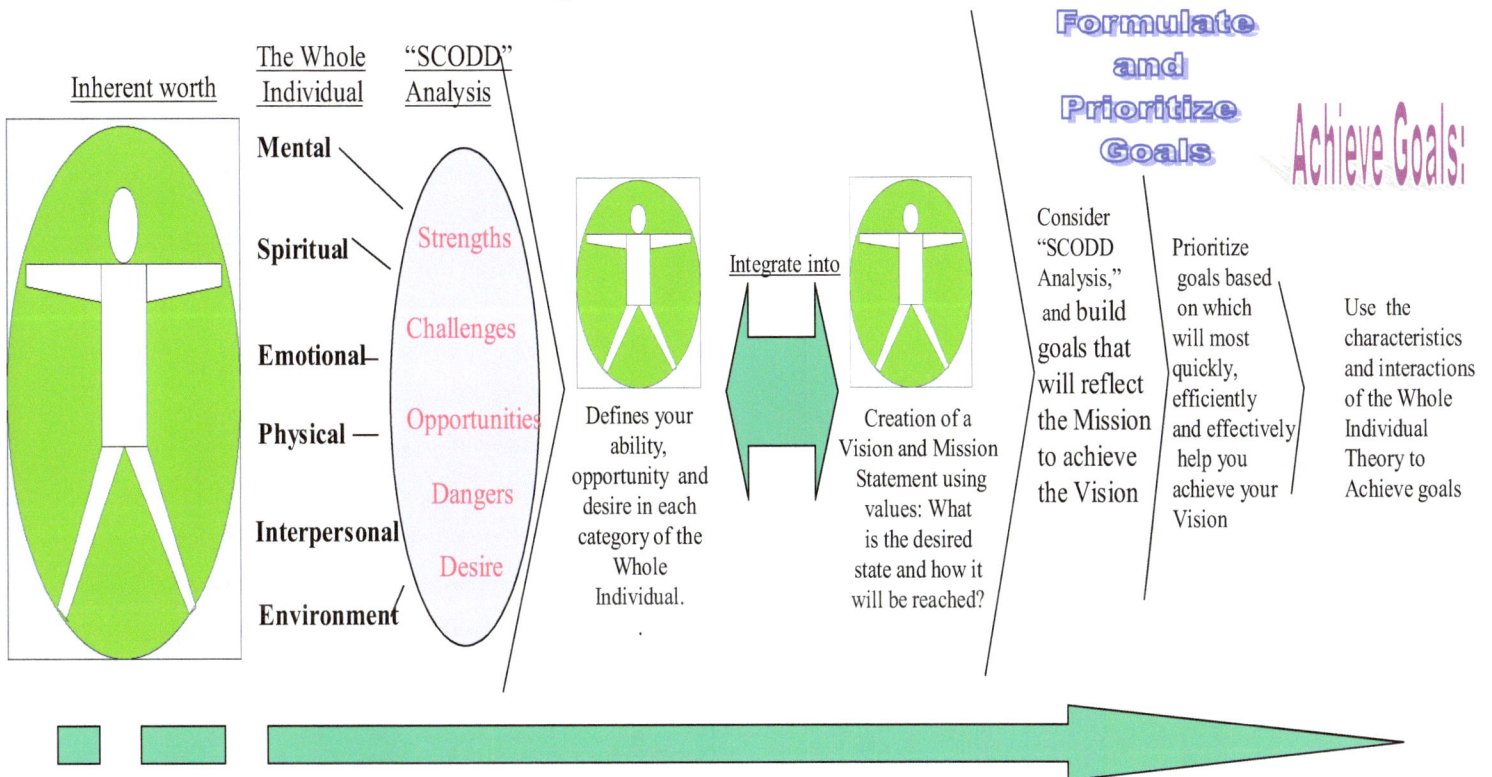

Inherent worth

The Whole Individual

"SCODD" Analysis

**Mental**

**Spiritual**

**Emotional**

**Physical**

**Interpersonal**

**Environment**

Strengths

Challenges

Opportunities

Dangers

Desire

Defines your ability, opportunity and desire in each category of the Whole Individual.

Integrate into

Creation of a Vision and Mission Statement using values: What is the desired state and how it will be reached?

Formulate and Prioritize Goals

Achieve Goals:

Consider "SCODD Analysis," and build goals that will reflect the Mission to achieve the Vision

Prioritize goals based on which will most quickly, efficiently and effectively help you achieve your Vision

Use the characteristics and interactions of the Whole Individual Theory to Achieve goals

# Methods and Strategies

On the following pages are some methods that may be used to effectively leverage inherent characteristics and interactions to achieve success.

# Mental

- Achieve your goals, over and over again in your mind.

   –Envision accomplishing your short, intermdiate and long range goals and how it will be experienced mentally, emotionally, physically, spiritually, interpersonally and environmentally.

   –Relive the future accomplishment of your goals many times in your mind, thinking of the Mental, Emotional, Physical, Spiritual, Interpersonal, and Environmental content of the goal.

- Research-learn all you can about your goal.

   –Get all the information you can about your goal and how to achieve it.

- Learn about others who are successful.

   –Study those who have accomplished a similar or the same goal.

      1. Learn about their strategies and lifestyle.

      2. Find out about their strengths and triumphs and how they achieved them, as well as their challenges and setbacks and how they overcame them. Understand how they felt during these situations.

      3. Apply what you have learned to your own strategy.

4. Believe that you too can be successful.

- Repetition- learning and using pertinent principles.

    –Learn pertinent principles by repeating them in your mind.

    –Repeat positive statements in your mind- "I can do it!" "Everyday I am getting thinner!"

- Modeling

    –Learn about those who may be your model.

    –Observe those who are successful at what they do.

    –When watching those who are successful, try to analyze their techniques and learn how and when they apply them.

    –Speak with or have lessons with those who are successful.

- Keep a written record of your goals and your daily progress towards them.

    –Write down short term steps, intermediate and long-range goals.

    –Use a system that allows you to prioritize your goals.

    –Plan your days, including accomplishment of short-term steps.

    –Track the progress on your goals.

—Review and revamp goals periodically to make sure you are on track to accomplishing what you want.

-Make plans as if you will accomplish your goal.

# Emotional

- Imagine how you will feel when you accomplish your goal.

    –Think often about how you will feel emotionally when you achieve your goal.

- Listen to motivational speakers.

    -A variety of seminars are presented throughout metropolitan areas on a variety of subjects.

    -Motivational downloads/CDs are available at local libraries and their websites.

    -You can purchase downloads/CDs from commercial websites and bookstores.

- Use inspirational material to keep you going.

    –Listen to inspirational music that reminds you of your dreams (such as music you listen to when you envision achieving your dreams) and motivates you to reach them.

    –Read inspirational literature.

    –Watch inspirational movies, programming.

- DESIRE!

    –Nourish a healthy yearning to achieve your goal.

- Direct emotions to productive channels.

–You have the choice to decide how you will act in certain situations.

–Negative emotions can be redirected into positive channels that will work toward the accomplishment of your purpose.

- Emotion charged learning.

    –Emotion combined with learning aids retention. Encoding principles or facts with positive emotional associations may help you to remember and recall them more effectively.

# Physical

- Good old fashioned WORK!

    –You can move a mountain one shovel at a time.

    –Many accomplish great things just because they work so hard to achieve them. It is not always because they are more talented, stronger or more intelligent than others.

- Intelligent work.

    –Much more can be accomplished when you find more intelligent or innovative ways to work.

    –Organize your work.

- Act as if you are who you want to be or have achieved what you desire.

    –Act as if you are already what you want to be or have accomplished your goals already.

    –Live as if you were your ideal person.

- Assimilate characteristics of successful individuals.

    –Assimilate character strengths of the person who has accomplished what you want.

- Success becomes a habit.

–The more short-term steps you achieve, the more you will gain confidence and expect success in attaining more difficult or longer range goals.

- Perfect practice, practice!

    –Practice must be technically and theoretically correct.

    –Frequent and consistent correct practice or work will make successful technique second nature.

# Spiritual

- Many have achieved marvelous things through spiritual conviction.

    – Many achieve things thought impossible through spiritual conviction and beliefs.

    - Spirituality may help you be more committed to your dreams.

- Draw upon a power greater than your own.

    - If you feel your goals are endorsed and encouraged by a higher power, it gives you a great feeling of support and motivation to achieve them.

    – Many gain more strength than their own through spirituality.

    – Spirituality gives strength to those who have exceeded their natural capabilities to continue towards their goal.

- Gain insight, enlightenment and direction.

    – Many gain ideas, enlightenment, and a sense of direction through spirituality.

    – Allows you to see different perspectives, not just based on physical drives, logic or emotions.

    – Inspires out of the box thinking.

- Relieve stress.

    –When you depend on a power greater than your own, it enables you to be relieved of the pressure to only rely on yourself. This allows you to perform at optimal levels.

- Prioritize

    –Spirituality may help you remember what is most important and thus help you prioritize goals.

    –Spirituality may help you not lose sight of other things (kindness to others, importance of family, charity work, philanthropy, etc.) that may help you live a more rounded life, and be more effective.

- Prayer, Introspection and meditation.

    –Inspiration may provide insight on your strengths, gifts, and opportunities as well as challenges and dangers.

    –Prayer, introspection and meditation may open new perceptions or insights to the world not before recognized. This may allow you to think of new and different ways to accomplish goals.

# Interpersonal

- Teamwork!

  –Working together towards a common goal allows for the accomplishment of more than the work of just one.

  –The whole is greater than the sum of its parts.

- Build a supportive network.

  –Surround yourself with positive people that believe in you and will support you in your goals.

  –Support others in the accomplishment of their goals.

- If possible, avoid consistent overly negative people.

  –Although you should never return aggression for negative treatment, or be rude, you should not pay much attention to non-constructive negative comments or behavior meant to demean your goals or cause you to believe you cannot achieve them. If possible avoid people who consistently engage in this type of communication or behavior.

  –Criticism should be constructive in nature and meant to build relationships.

  –Help those who are negative to become more positive, if possible.

- The amazing power of genuine compliments and kindness.

–Kindness softens resistance, "you attract more flies with honey than vinegar."

–Thoughtful words make others feel better about themselves and more apt to help you.

–Compliments must be genuine, sincere.

–Thoughtfulness encourages positive behavior.

–Appreciation for others engenders cooperation, teamwork and synergy.

–The ability to see and communicate the good in others builds interpersonal relationship skills.

- Altruism- helps others achieve their goals.

    –Helping others helps you to feel good about yourself and may build confidence and personal power.

    –Many believe what you send out will come back to you; the person you help may be the person that helps you or others you love later.

    –You learn much and become more experienced by helping others.

- Respect with disagreement.

    –Respect for others and their beliefs, even if they are different from your own, allows you to maintain working relationships that may prove mutually beneficial or complimentary in the future.

—Respecting others with beliefs other than your own, allows you to stay open-minded and understand how others view life. This allows you to broaden your horizons, be more knowledgeable and foster interpersonal relations helpful in accomplishing goals.

1. One example is appreciating another's culture, which may cultivate business relations.

-Maintaining respectful relationships with those who have different views keeps the door open for them to consider and possibly accept your views sometime in the future.

- Associate with those who have achieved similar goals or have the same ambition.

   —Camaraderie can be built among those striving for the same goals. This can strengthen and encourage all involved.

   —Those working towards similar ends can share effective techniques and strategies that will help others succeed.

- Be sensitive to others after accomplishment of goals.

   —Others' feelings of self worth may be threatened when you accomplish your goal. This may especially be true if they have not achieved all that they would like. Be sensitive to this.

   —Include others in your victory.

   —Show appreciation for those who helped you and kindness for those who have not accomplished what you have - emphasize their achievements.

# Environmental

- Environmental cues and reinforcement.

    –Use images, symbols and written statements that will remind you of your goal and reinforce it in your mind.

- Attraction of desired goals.

    –When you create your goals in your mind and commit to achieve them, you will draw what you desire to you, or propel yourself to what you wish to achieve.

- You can change your environment to your advantage.

- Organize your environment and workspace.

- Create an environment that is conducive to the accomplishment of goals.

    –Remove negative cues and reinforcements.

    –Remove temptations to fail and distractions.

    –Set up your environment with tools to accomplish your goals.

        1. Comfortable chair and computer to write a book.

- Use available resources in your environment.

    –Learn to adapt to the environment in which you will accomplish your goals.

1. The Army trains in the desert and uses the desert to their advantage.

2. The chameleon and other animals use their environment to survive.

–Learn about resources in your environment.

1. Classes, libraries, clubs, etc. may provide resources to help you.

2. Many scholarships go unused because no one searches them out.

–Make use of what is around you.

1. Great athletes run up and down mountains or use other tools inherent in their environment to gain strength and endurance as well as develop skills.

-Turn obstacles into opportunities and Resources.

1. Learn to take obstacles in your path towards your goal, and view them in a different, positive light. Take the opportunity to think of innovative ways to turn obstacles into resources that will help you to succeed.

2. Sometimes failure or rejection can be used as motivation to work harder to achieve goals.

• Learn how your characteristics effectively work together and in conjunction with your interactions so that you can manage them in a useful way.

–Interrelationships between your characteristics and their interactions with others and the environment may be somewhat complex and could present challenges. Being aware of this and understanding such relationships is vital to learning how to effectively manage them towards productivity.

–Objectiveness and innovative thinking are essential when considering how to manage the intricate interrelationships between your own characteristics and interactions.

-Developing productive interrelationships will foster synergistic strengths and provide great personal power.

# References

Carnegie, D. (author), Pell, A.R., & Carnegie, D. (editors). (1982). <u>How to Win Friends and Influence People.</u> New York: Simon and Schuster.

Carnegie, D. (author), & Carnegie, D. (editor). (1984) <u>How to Stop Worrying and Start Living.</u> New York: Simon and Schuster.

Covey, S. (1989) <u>The Seven Habits of Highly Effective People.</u> New York: Simon and Schuster.

"Quotations Database" <u>Motivational Quotes.com Web Site</u> June 2001. Online http://www.motivationalquotes.com

Devore, S. (1984) <u>The Neuropsychology of Achievement.</u> Audio book Newark, CA: Sybervision Systems incorporated.

Ziglar, Z. (1998) <u>Breaking Through to the Next Level.</u> Tulsa,OK: Honor Books.

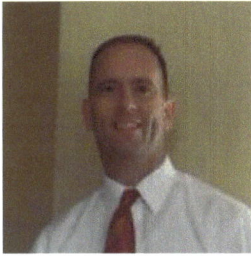

## About the author

Scott Newberger learned about setting and achieving goals at an early age when he decided he wanted to try out for the high school football team, although he had never played any organized sports. He had been heavy set as a boy and was always picked last during any athletic endeavors. Through his faith in God and with the help of friends and family, Scott was excited to reach his goal and made the second of two freshman football teams, even though he was last string. Prayers and hard work helped him improve and by the end of the year he was starting. Eventually he started on varsity and became the captain of the high school football team.

This and other events helped Scott to believe that dreams can be achieved. He also learned the process that allows success.

Scott is currently the President and CEO of Lifecharge Consulting, a firm dedicated to strategic coaching for organizations and individuals. He is a portfolio consultant for a major brokerage firm and sits on the Board of Directors for R. W. Meyer Company, one of the largest privately owned land management companies in Hawaii. Scott has a Masters in Business Administration, a Masters in Innovative Leadership, a Bachelors Degree in Psychology and is an Accredited Asset Management Specialist.

Scott is also a member of the Arizona Air National Guard where he's been involved in project management and has been a certified trainer and instructor. He enjoys teaching and has spoken in front of hundreds. He holds a College Teaching Certificate and has taught Community College of the Air Force Certified Classes.

During his free time Scott enjoys spending time with his wife and children. He is an Elder in The Church of Jesus Christ of Latter-Day Saints where he works as a youth leader. Scott is a Black Belt in Karate and is a Certified Sports Mental Training Coach.

Through Lifecharge PowerPac © and Lifecharge Organizational PowerPac ©, Scott wishes to help individuals and organizations reach their full potential. He believes through proper analysis and strategic goal setting, higher levels of achievement can be attained than had afore been considered possible.

www.ingramcontent.com/pod-product-compliance
Lightning Source LLC
LaVergne TN
LVHW072106070426
835509LV00002B/45